We Ride

Jan Swartz

Illustrated by Dennis Strand

Dominie Press, Inc.

Publisher: Raymond Yuen
Series Editor: Stanley L. Swartz
Consultant: Adria F. Klein
Editor: Bob Rowland
Designers: Lois Stanfield and Vincent Mao
Illustrator: Dennis Strand

First published 1997
New Edition © 2002 Dominie Press, Inc.

Published by:

🖋 **Dominie Press, Inc.**

1949 Kellogg Avenue
Carlsbad, California 92008 USA

www.dominie.com

ISBN 1-56270-706-X

Printed in Singapore by PH Productions Pte Ltd
1 2 3 4 5 6 PH 03 02 01

ITP

He rides in a car.

She rides in a truck.

He rides in a wagon.

She rides in a cab.

He rides in a van.

She rides in a jeep.

He rides on a motorcycle.

We ride in a bus.